w h i s p e r s

passionate poetry and words of love
from first glance to lasting romance

by

Thena Smith

Edited by Linda LaTourelle

Bluegrass PUBLISHING

www.theultimateword.com
270·251·3600

For information write:
Blue Grass Publishing
PO Box 634
Mayfield, KY 42066 USA
service@theultimateword.com
www.theultimateword.com
www.bluegrasspublishing.com

ISBN: 0-9761925-8-6

1st ed.
Mayfield, KY : Blue Grass Pub., 2005

Cover Design: Todd Jones, Tennessee
Proudly printed in the United States of America

10 9 8 7 6 5 4 3 2 1

Table of Contents

Whispers-Words of Love

What word stirs our emotions more than the word love? Poets write of it and singers sing of it while artists try to capture it in stone, plaster, paint or multiple other mediums. All of us want it and treasure it.

Young people think of the more physical part of love but as we mellow and mature we appreciate the lasting love that is deeply embedded in our hearts and souls. We no longer search for the person with the hunky body but the kind heart and kindred spirit.

In this little book I want to include poems for the young person who is experiencing that first love, the person about to be married and the more mature of age who are celebrating milestone anniversaries as well as those starting over with a new romance.

It is my prayer that with each verse I share you receive a blessing in the form of truth, beauty, wisdom or humor and that it helps you to appreciate even more the wonder that is love!

Dedication

Dedicated to my Heavenly Father from whom I received the husband I adore and our wonderful daughter. He is the giver of every perfect gift of love.

Whisper

Whisper words of love to me
When you are near by
Tell me that you love me
And then please tell me why.

Whisper little secrets
That are just for me
Whisper little saucy things
And my smile you'll see.

Whisper that you love me
And will always love me true
And I will whisper back
Sweet loving words to you!

Whisper words of love to me
Soft and sweet, so tenderly!

Romance and Flirtations

A Serious Flirtation

There are those who would say
That a flirtation in any way
Is nothing of good intent
And speaks of interest
Casual and not well meant...
While others love to play the game
And as a result wear another's name
From that casual glance
That wink of an eye
The touch of a dainty foot
Came an interest so sweet and true
That love and romance came shining through
Filling each life with matrimonial bliss
And all from that first flirtatious kiss...

Flirtations:

That wink of an eye

The touch of a dainty foot

A whisper so soft!

Once upon a time

Once upon a time
A long time ago
There was a romantic evening and
by a candle's warm glow
A woman declared her love
To her sweetheart true
And realized her prince
Had come at last
And that prince was
...you.

This Rose Means I Love You

This rose means I love you
And will my whole life through
This rose is a sign
Of my undying love for you.
This rose brings kisses
From my lips to you
Keep these petals with you
If you love me too.

I love the way you look at me

I love the way you smile

I love the way you make me feel

So special all the while!

When We Met

One day we met
And the earth stood still
The emotions I felt
I feel them still...

Suddenly the sky
Seemed bluer than blue
And the rose's scent
Was not as sweet as you..

The mighty ocean
Seemed not as big as before
Because you were in my arms
To love and adore...

So many, many things
Changed that day
Because wonderful you
Came into my life to stay!

You make my heart sing
As no one else can do!

A Smile for You

Look at me and see this smile.
Which is meant for you
For you brighten my day
And make my heart sing
As no one else can do!

Roses and Stuff

Some guys send roses
In a vase of gold
Not just one rose
But all a vase can hold.

Others send candy
The best to be found
Not just a few morsels
But confections by the pound.

Some can afford jewelry
To wear on the wrist
And others think cars
Would hold a girl's interest.

But even if you were rich and debonair
And could affords tiaras
To decorate my hair
It couldn't outshine
The love that we share!

Dear Sweetheart,

You are looking spiffy today
And I love the way you smell
Your eyes sparkle like diamonds
I love you, can you tell?

A Little Bit of Romance

I need a bit of romance
A tiny hint of love
A tangible bit of attention
From the one I'm dreaming of....

I need a touch on the shoulder
Or a pat upon my cheek
And perhaps a glance my way
When I begin to speak.

I need to see that I'm presentable
To the one that is the object of my crush
Just to know they know my name
Would give me quite a rush!

I am so in love with everything-

Well, everything that's you!

One Little Word

You give me goose bumps
My breath comes in gasps
My mind goes suddenly blank
And I have a brain relapse!

I feel as if I've eaten chocolate
Or had the very finest wine
I see the sun and stars and moon
All at the very same time.

What is it that causes me
To get that blush and glow?
Oh, it only takes a smile from you
And one little soft "hello".

I Need You

Sometimes the night seems really long
Before the daylight comes again
I need great big giant hugs and kisses
To last me until then!

Your Love is
Written on My Heart!

Our Story

I felt shy and out of place
And I loved you from afar
Watching you with your friends after work
As you zoomed off in your car.

The other girls looked at you
And gave you nods and winks
And I just watched you flirt with them
Offering to buy them drinks.

I never thought I would measure up
And catch your eye at all
So imagine what a surprise it was
When you decided to call.

I think you knew that I was the one
Right from the very start
For you weren't one for superficial looks
But saw right into my heart.

I was so excited to be with you
And you seemed to like me as well
Things worked out so wonderfully right
And that's why we have a story to tell!

Love is the Music the Heart Makes

Love is the Music that the heart sings
And its music has sweetest tune around
If you are attuned and listen carefully
You can hear its lovely sound.
Love has a gentle rhythmic whisper
That those who know love recognize
Love rejoices with those who are happy
And with sadness, love will sympathize.
Love has a gentle cadence.
That lifts the sprit of those we hold dear
For love's song was first designed in Heaven
And sung by the angels as they hovered near.
Love's song has sweetness and a softness
That never wants to cause hurt or distress
And love that is returned from one heart to another
Well, this type of love is just the very best.
Oh, how I love the music that I hear
Played in my heart and soul today
I pray that I will always be able to hear it
And that my heart, its music will always play!
Instruments created by the best musicians
That will ever tread upon this earthly sod
Can only get a minuscule measure of the perfection
Of music created by the heart of God.

Love is the music that makes the heart sing!

Love On-Line

I found my wonderful
And special valentine
When I was searching
For love online.

Never did I think how special
Surfing the internet could be
Until I found the perfect match
A Valentine for me!

You are the world's best hubby
And I'm thankful that you're mine
And I'm thankful for the internet
And for romancing done online!!

Some Loves have a dot.com

Through the modern Internet
My wonderful sweetie and I met
Though I said that I would never succumb
To looking for romance through a dot.com
One day I found him signing on
And I knew then my heart was gone!

www.loveonlineyouandi.com

World Wide Web

You could get on the internet
And search the whole world through
But never find another sweetheart
That is half as great as you!

You could go to the museum
And search back into historic time
And never find a man as wonderful
As this man of mine.

You could go into outer space
You could sail the ocean blue---
I guess what I am trying to say is
I'm glad that my sweetheart is YOU!

Is there Love Online?

You can really truly
Find love on line
I know it's true
For I found mine!
He was there
When I logged on
And before I knew it
My heart was gone!

Love on the line!

If You Love Me...

If you love me
Tell me please
And tell me right away.
Don't worry about the setting
Or the proper words to say...
If you really care for me
Let me know you do.
Let me hear the words
From the heart of you...
If you value my friendship
And my life you want to share
Tell me that I'm special
And those tender feelings share.
Don't feel embarrassed or inhibited
Or think it might seem odd
For love and friendship are gifts
Right from the Hand of God.
If you love me let me know it
And I will treasure every word
For loving sentiments from the lips
By the heart are heard.

This love of mine...

Oh how fine, simply divine!

How Much Do I Love You?

If you would ask me how much I love you
I would have to say I do not know
For each day that I am with you
That love tends to grow!

If you ask me why I love you
I could not tell you why
It would be like asking me
To describe the sky!

I love you when we are together
And I love you when we are apart.
For you are always with me
As close as my beating heart.

Your gentleness made you my friend

Your compassion made you my confidant

Your strength in adversity made you my hero

But your loving heart made you my husband.

You Are As Close As My Heart

Some may say that we are far away
And how can our love be true
But no matter how many the miles between us
My heart feels close to you.

We were friends first
And liked each other from the start
For instantly you were recognized
As someone special by my heart.

As time passed our friendship grew
And grew and grew and then
We realized that we were sweethearts
Where once we had been dear friends.

So dear sweetheart I am sharing
My heart and soul with you
And in this verse is a special kiss
Straight from my heart to you!

Love Is a Gift

When I receive a gift from you
It's as special as can be
But the greatest gift I already have
The love you share with me!

You Melt My Heart

When I look into your eyes
I often am surprised
At all of the love I see
Reflected back to me.

When I look at your dear face
And when I feel the warmth
of your embrace
My heart is filled with love
And my fears are all erased.

When your lips meet mine
It's as if our hearts entwine
I know the two of us will never part
Because you stir my soul and
You melt my heart.

Innocent Flirtation

It began as a flirtation
Just an innocent little look
As I saw that you were reading
My very favorite book.
It began with a little nod your way
And then the most casual little glance
Became the initiation
Of a wonderful romance!

Isn't It Romantic

Isn't it romantic
To stand upon the shore
Listening to the music
Of the ocean's roar?

Isn't it romantic
With the sand beneath our feet
To hear in the quietness
Your own true love's heartbeat?

Oh I love the ocean
I love to stand upon the shore
I love the glow of moonlight
But I love you even more!

Oh, How I Love Romance!

I love to sing and be sung to
I love the joy of the dance
I love to be loved by the one I love
And oh, how I love romance!

I love the constant attention
Of candy and flowers and such
I enjoy the thrill and forever I will
The thrill of being romanced!

Love Letters

I wrote a long love letter
I wrote it all by hand
But at the end of the day
It was washed away
For I wrote it in the sand.

I wrote another letter
I wrote it on the wall
Right beside the telephone
So that I could read it as I called.

But when I went to call you
The wall had been washed clean
I think the janitor did it
Just trying to be mean!

But I wrote another letter
And I meant each special part
No one can ever erase it
For I wrote it in my heart!

Love and Sand

Don't write love letters in the sand
For at the end of a perfect day
The tide will rush in
And your love will be washed away!

Ah, Romance

If you find a man who is romantic
You should latch onto him
For guys usually do romantic things
Only on a whim.

If you find a guy who sings to you
Grab on and hold him tight
For of romantic love songs
Most men have a fright!

And if he says "I love you"
Whatever else you do
Hold his hand
Look into his eyes
And say "I love you too!"

Love is Even Better

Being in love is even better
than being in like
One is a sports car
The other a bike!

Isn't it romantic?

I Love You

This morning you said "I love you"
When you spoke my name.
You didn't add those three little words
But I heard it just the same!

You said I love you with your smile
At least that's what I heard.
I read it in your smiling face
Even though you didn't say the word.

At noon you said I love you
When you hugged me by surprise
It made so sweetly happy
That tears formed in my eyes!

Tonight you said I love you
And how sweet to hear you say
The three little words "I love you"
Although I heard them
throughout the day!

Flowers bloom along our path

We know God put them there

And as long as flowers bloom

This true love we will share.

Being With You

Do you know my
Favorite thing to do?
My favorite thing
Is being with you!

My favorite place
That I like to be
Is right beside you
With you beside me!

My favorite song
That I like to sing
Together with you
Is any old thing!

My favorite house
Can be any kind
As long as the house
Is both yours and mine!

My favorite person
You are, you see
And next to you
Is where I love to be!

My favorite thing...

is you!

Paradise

What paradise is this,
What place have I found
That makes me smile in awe
As my feet tread upon its ground.
I walked on wondering about this bliss
And then I knew it was true
That Paradise could be any place
That I could share with you!

The Depth of My Love

Can you count the grains of sand
That decorate the shore
If you could count their number
I would still love you even more.

Is there a number of the times
A wave can come crashing onto the beach
Or is there a limit to the seaweed
That gets washed within our reach?

Can you count the rays of sunshine
That shine down on us from above
If so, then you have a place to start
To tell you the depth of my love.

My Heart Has Found Its Home in You

My Heart has found its home in you
And once nestled in your arms
Nothing else would do.
My heart wants only you.

My eyes have found their resting place
And once my arms found your embrace
My eyes just could not leave your face.
My eyes see only you.

My ears have found the sound they love
Your voice is like music from above
My ears love to hear the sound of your voice so dear.
My ears hear only you.

My soul mate you are and always shall be
For my heart is full of love you see
I will love you faithfully and true,
For my heart has found its home in you.

Home Sweet Home

I have found my own sweet home
And I intend to stay
Contentedly with my true love
And never go away.

Engagement

So You're Engaged!

So you're engaged
And soon will be wed
I celebrate with you this happy day
And all the days that are ahead.

As you look forward to the future
And as your life together you begin
I pray that you will always love each other
And that you will be the best of friends.

May you always be as happy
As you are on this special day
And may you treat each other gently
In all you do and all you say.
It won't be long until your wedding day
And all these preparations will be past
Enjoy each blissful wedding moment
For the time will go so fast.

Years will pass by quickly
With your true love at your side
And you will remember with misty eyes
The day you became a bride!

So happy together!

A Promise for My Love

A ring is a promise
Of what is yet to be
With this ring I ask you
To promise your heart to me...

I do not take it lightly
That you trust me with your heart
I will treat it gently
Each and every part.

Some must search their whole lives through
To find a love that is pure and true
But we were blessed beyond compare
To find the love which we now share.

Accept this promise and this ring
As we wait to see what the future will bring.
Whether there be storms or fair weather
My fondest dream is that we share it together.

Dreams do come true

For my love I found you!

Our Engagement

What a happy day it was
When you asked me to marry you!
I knew you were my hero
And my dream come true.
For I dreamed about a soul mate
That would love me as I am inside
And whose heart's desire
Would be to have me as his bride.
I loved you as a friend
And came to depend on you
But soon I realized
I had fallen in love with you.
And then came the engagement
How lovely and how thrilling
To wear the ring upon my finger
Of the man who my dreams would be fulfilling.
How I looked forward to that day
When we would become as one
Then I knew I would be complete
When our life together had begun.

From this moment on

A new hope has begun!

Blind Dates

No More Blind Dates

Do you remember blind dates
From so many years ago?
Do they still have those?
Does anybody know?

I remember walking out
To meet my handsome date
I saw him through the doorway
And I could hardly wait!

His hair was short and dark
And his eyes were black as night.
His shoulders were broad and sturdy
And he was a handsome sight.

Well, I thought to myself
It's not been bad so far
Until he spoke these words...
"Your date is in the car..."

Blind in Love or is it

Love is Blind?

The World of Us

Fondly I sit here and look
At photos for our special book
And I think of how you enrich my day
In such a loving and special way!
You have brought like a shinning sun
Into my life such joy and fun
I enjoy all that you say and do
And cherish the specialness of you!
Once I was content to be just me
And I thought I was happy as could be
But it seems that now, all I discuss
Is the wonderful thrill of the world of US!

Your Smile

What could be
Precious to me
And what am I
Most anxious to see?
What can brighten
The darkest day
What can chase
Storm clouds away?
What will I remember
Until I'm 103?
It's the way
You smile at me!

I Could Be Happy

I could be happy with an older car
Or a house that needed repair.
I could be happy in a trailer
As long as you were there.

I could be happy with lack of funds
Or bills that were past due
I could live in a rickety rackety house
If I lived there with you.

I could take the bus to get around
To do my chores or go to town
Or I could use a trolley to travel
As long as our love didn't unravel.

Most things I really don't need
As for riches I crave very few
There's only one thing I can't do without....
I could never do without YOU!

Forty Reasons Why I Love You

Forty reasons why I love you
Would only be a start
For I have a million reasons
Stored safely in my heart-

My Heart Remembers You

*Although I have not seen you
In quite a while
I treasure your friendship
And remember your smile.*

*I remember your excitement
At things that were new
And the fun times I had
Hanging around with you.*

*Miles have separated us
And time has not stood still
But I wanted to send a hello note
For my heart remembers you still!*

Us

*You are still You
And I am still me
But after all the
hustle and bustle and fuss
You and I become We
And married we'll be...
And then we become "US"*

You and me—Just the two of Us!

Anniversary

Only God's timing could be so perfect
And could have brought to me
The one whose heart
Fitted with mine so perfectly!

Still Dancing

Look at them as they glide across the floor
Has it been 50 years ...or is it more
That they have moved in this special way
Each one in tune with the other's sway.
Resting and relaxing in the arms of each other
Secure and confident of their love and caring
This moment listening to and lost in the music
They are so sweetly sharing.
How I love the look of the two of them
As the glide across the floor
Even with a Fred and Ginger
You could not ask for more.
For this is love that has maturity
This is love with beauty and grace
This is love that has lasted through the years
And is reflected on each precious face.

May Your Love Only Grow Sweeter

May your love only grow sweeter
Through the passing years
May your heart be full of laughter
And only joy filled tears.
May you always love each other
Just as much as today and more
And enjoy all the wonder
That your lives hold in store.

Thanking God for His Love for You!

I am so grateful to God above
That He brought to my dear friends
Such deep and enduring love.
So thankful that He looked inside each heart
And knew you belonged together
From time's very start.
For before the earth was formed
I believe God created in each of you
Those special qualities
Which would form this love so true.
Only God's timing could be so perfect
And only those who trust Him will understand
The perfection in His purpose
And the guiding of His hand!
As we who love you both
Celebrate this love with you
We ask for God to bless this special day
And each day your whole lives through.

Renewing my Vows to You

Fifty years ago when we were wed
Sweet and loving vows we said
I promised that my whole life through
To you my love, I would be true.

Years have gone by
And I still feel
That the love we share
Is just as real.

We have shared the good times
As well as the bad
We have celebrated in happy times
And clung together in the sad.

We have become closer each year
Becoming more "us" and "we"
Growing closer every day
And feeling less, just "you" or "me."

I have no problem with wondering
Just where I stop and you begin
For 50 years ago I married my soul mate
My sweetheart and my best friend.

And with no hesitation in my heart
I cherish the renewal of my vow to you
To love you and cherish you my love
And spend the rest of my lifetime with you!

For Mom and Dad

You have been such a wonderful
And loving couple for 25 years
Sharing the happy times where laughter echoed
And the sad times with their share of tears.
You have been there for each other
While you have shared a love so true
That has been a treasure to each other
And blessed those about you too!
I have a little gift for you.
This little ginkgo tree.
Which I offer it as a tangible symbol
Of what stability should be.
I hope that each time you look at it
You feel happiness through and though
For like the faithful ginkgo tree
I see that loving stability in you.
May your years continue to be happy
And your love remain strong and true
May love and laughter fill your life each day
And each day may God bless you!
I am so glad to be your daughter
And each day I thank God above
For choosing two parents for me
Whose hearts were so full of love!

Happy Anniversary!!

I Will Love You Forever

I will love you forever
And loving words will always say
And if I forget, please remind me
To tell you every day!

Seven Years of Happiness

Seven years of happiness
Seven years of fun
I love you even more today
Than when we had just begun.

Change the years to reflect the anniversary!

Love Messages in a Bottle

A Message in A Bottle

I found a message in a bottle
That had washed up on the shore
I wondered about the writer
... if they were watching for it still
As the bottle was tossed to and fro
At the ocean's will.
I found a message in a bottle
And it inspired me to write one too
I sealed it up so nice and tight
And sent it via ocean mail to you.

A Message in A Bottle

If I had lived 100 years ago
And we had only just met
I would not have email
Or the modern Internet.

But to tell you of my love
I would find a way
And I would tell you somehow
How you are the sunshine in my day.

I would put a message in a bottle
And toss it into the sea
Trusting that somehow my love
You would get that note from me! -
or
I found a message in a bottle
Written so many years ago
By someone so much in love
With a sweetheart that didn't know.
I resolved when I saw it
That one thing I would forever do
Is to let you know, my darling
That I'm so in love with you! -

One message—simply love!

A Message in A Bottle

Don't keep your feelings bottled up
Let your loved ones know how you feel
And that you treasure them
With a love heart felt and real!
You can toss a bottle into the sea
And wait for many a year
While loved ones wait at home alone
Fighting back a lonely tear.
And if someday the waves should roll
And wash that bottle on shore
There is always the possibility
That they are waiting there no more! -

Here's a Message...

Here's a message in a bottle
That speaks so quietly to you
It says my heart is happy
And that my love is true.

I put it in this bottle
So it would last eternally
Carried out by rolling waves
Into the deep blue sea.

Someday, someone will find it
And it will tell them that I cared
And they will get just a little hint
Of the deep love we shared.

Key to My Heart

The key to my heart
Is a precious thing
Given only to a chosen few.
But it only took a little while
To know it belonged to you.
So, dear one here is my heart
For you alone with the key I trust
I am handing the key to my heart to you
And treat it gently you must.

You Hold the Key to My Heart

You hold the key to my heart
Please treat it tenderly
It is unique and can't be replaced
And you hold the only key!

What is time?

It is moments made of gold
When you have the hand
Of someone you love to hold.
It is for life and living
It is for sharing and being and giving.
Time is precious
And it is so true
That it is never more precious
Than when I'm sharing it with you.

Together We Walk Into Our Future

Side by side and hand in hand
We walk into our future
No longer two alone but two together
Promising each other to love and nurture
Be it fair sky or stormy weather.
Today we walk out into love, light and beauty
With gentle skies and balmy sunlit air
We are surrounded by those who love us
Happiness and laughter are everywhere.
But our promises of love will be enduring
No matter what life will hold in store
And with each step we take into our future
I promise I will only love you more!

I Fell in Love in Autumn

Autumn comes so gently
With nature's paintbrush in its hands
It only whispers gentle things
And never makes demands.

First a little streak of red
A little streak of gold
And then the brown takes over
By the time the weather's cold.

Continued next page...

Continued from previous page...

I fell in love in the Autumn time
As nature perfected its lovely art
You came so sweetly into my life
And stole away my heart.

I knew in the Autumn I loved you
And knew that the whole year through
I would look back with fondness
On the day I knew I loved you.

Honeymooners

Cooking at You

Cooking at you gives my heart a lift
You are a rare and precious gift.
I look in your eyes and in them I see
Reflected right back
Is your love for me.

Being with you is my heart's desire
It feels as if our love is a fire
Which burns so bright and strong and true
Telling the world that I love you!

Here's looking at you darling!

The Heart Doesn't Speak In fancy Words

The heart doesn't speak in fancy words
That only learned men can understand
But speaks in soft and gentle sighs
And touches of the hand

The heart speaks in glances sweet and loving
And tender gentle kisses
It speaks in such subtle ways
That sometimes their voice a person misses

The heart speaks in gentle thoughts
That cause a loving act
A gentle touch upon the head
Or a pat upon the back.

Poets through the ages
From the dawn of man
With their pen have expounded on the feelings
Instilled by the simplest touch of the human hand.

The tiniest baby knows of love
And needs not the poets word
For he is shown the power of love
By every each tender coo he's heard.

For those whose tongues cannot express
In eloquent poetry or stylish prose
Their love song for our Lord above
He sees your heart and knows.

The Beach Awaits

In Jamaica in a cove
On the lovely sandy shore
Sits a lonely beach chair
I could not miss it more...

I found so much peace and happiness
As I sat in that lovely place
And looked out to the point in the distance
Loving the wind and sun upon my face.

Ah, the sound of water
As it lapped upon the beach
And the things of comfort
Were still within my reach...

Oh, I long so to go back to Jamaica
I made such lovely memories there
In my mind I go there frequently
And find my still waiting chair.

Our Honeymoon

Our honeymoon was unique
The cabin was old and quaint
It had no hot water
And it lacked of paint.

Our little car was old
And the little car was tired
And to get us there
It worked so very hard.

Continued next page

45

Continued previous page

Our luggage was hand me down
And we were on a break from school
We were so excited to be wed
Wow! We thought we were cool.

We laughed and smiled at each other
In a brand new special way
It was as if the word had no words
For what we wanted to say.

There was no orchestra to play
No wine and fancy place to dine
Just a lasting pledge of love
From your heart and from mine.

Your First Christmas Together

If Christmas has always been wonderful
A time cherished and special to see
Sharing your first Christmas together
Will show you how lovely it can be.
Each bough of the tree becomes important
Each light and each ornament so fine
Reminds you of your love for each other
And love and tenderness in your faces shine.
This is your first "married" Christmas
And so lovely is the sweet memory
That I know you look forward to the coming years
So you can see just how marvelous it will be! --Thena

You are Loved

The Christmas season
Has a special reason
It reminds us of God's love
That he would send His Son to earth
In a simple stable birth
This time causes us to reflect
On those who are so dear
And tell them of the love in our hearts
That we feel for them all year!
This card is to tell you
That you mean so much to me
And I hope that my actions
This love you could always see.
But in case you didn't know it
I'm setting the record straight
I love you very much dear spouse
And your life I celebrate!

Gift for My Sweetheart

For my sweetheart
The love of my life
My wonderful and beautiful
Much loved wife...
The kids have been fed
I've tucked them in and turned out the light.
So please put on what's inside this box
And join me for a romantic night!

Nothing Short of My Everything

You're nothing short of my everything
And make me just a bit shy
When I look at you and realize
That you are my handsome guy!

You are my very best friend
Who knows me through and through
And I am so in love with everything-
Well, everything that's you!

All of me—you can have all of me!

Story Poems

An Old Story Revisited

Their love was strong and true
And their lives were simple and sweet
But as for funds they had barely enough
To keep them off the street.

Christmas time was coming
And no gifts had they to share
It made each of the couple sad
It was more they either could bear.

I'll sell my watch thought he
And bought a present for his wife
He could just see the lovely hair ornament
On his joy, his love, his life!

And she who loved her husband so
Walked miles out in the cold and snow
And sold her lovely long brown hair
Just so his Christmas joy she could share.

Continued next page

Continued previous page

This chain she thought sweetly to herself
Will not stay upon a shelf
But I can hardly wait to see his face
As he sees what chain his watch will grace.

And soon it was the time to show
And give the gifts they had to share
When she noticed that he had no watch
And he that she had no hair...

This Rose Means I Love You

It was in an envelope
Yellow and crumpled with age
A note Written in a lovely old-fashioned script
That gracefully filled the page.
This rose means I love you
And will my whole life through
This rose is a tangible sign
Of my undying love for you.
This rose brings kisses
From my lips to you
Keep these petals with you
If you love me true.
And should we never met again
And fate keeps us apart
Keep at least one petal
And wear it near your heart.
What happened to those lovers
Whose lips once kissed this rose?
What happened to their love story
How can I find someone who knows?
Oh, I pray they are together
And time has been so kind
For a love so sweet and tender
Is so very rare to find!
My love for you is just as precious
Just as sweet and true
So I've kissed each petal on this rose
And I'm sending it to you.

Most Wonderful Time

The most wonderful time of your life is now
Even if sometimes you worry about how
You will get through tough times and such
But these are the days that you feel and touch!
This is the most wonderful time in your History
Even if sometimes it seems like a mystery
And you think of things you wish you could do-
But this is the day that belongs to you!
These may not be the best days as far as wealth
Or perhaps you have problems with your health
But this is the day that you have in the palm of your hand
The day when you can triumph or make a stand...
This is the day when you can call on a friend
Or perhaps there's a card or letter you need to send?
This is the time you can hug someone-
Perhaps a husband or daughter or son.
You have those treasured memories of the past
And you know that time goes by too fast
So this is the day when it is up to you
To do those things you know you should do.
Yes, this day is the best day of your life
Because it is the day you have to live
The day you have to love, laugh, and celebrate
And perhaps a day to forgive.

Memories—the legacy of love continues!

You Were the Answer to My Prayer

You were the answer to my prayer
You were my dream come true
I asked the Father for a miracle
And He sent me you!

You were the greatest gift
That I could ever crave
I asked God for a precious gift
And you were the gift He gave!

You were the reason that I could smile
You were the words to the songs I sang
I asked God for for a tune
And He gave me everything!

He gave me a reason to wake up each day
With someone to love and laugh and play
He gave me a reason to laugh and to smile
Making my life seem more worthwhile!

The days were sweet when we first met
And grew sweeter every day
You brought me such joy and happiness
And brought unbounded love my way!

And each night when I count my blessings
I thank the Father above
For answering my yearning hearts deepest prayer
And sending you for me to love!

Your Eyes

My sweetheart, your eyes are so bright
Sparkling like diamonds in the light
Filled with love and promise
And in everything seeing delight.

My darling, when I look into your eyes
My heart leaps from the love I feel
For I know that I look into your soul
And I can't believe this blessing can be real.

I pray that forever your eyes will be
Filled with the love and tenderness I see
And you will see that same immensity of love
Reflected back to you from the heart of me.

His Love

I believe the eyes are mirrors of the soul
And their tenderness we don't control.
I believe that God in Heaven above
Has filled your heart and soul
and your eyes reflect His love.

A heart of love—

is a gift from above!

For My Husband /Christmas/Valentine

In case you do not know
Or in case you can't see
How much I love you
And how dear you are to me...

You are my best friend
The music to my words of praise.
Only my calendar of life
You are my holidays!

You are the husband
That I always hoped I'd find.
You are my sweetheart always
You are my Valentine!

You are the reason for my being
You are the ornaments
On my Christmas tree
I am blessed beyond all measure
Having you to share your love with me!

Daisies Never Tell

I saw a daisy on the side of the street
A flower so dainty, so lovely and sweet
"Does he love me?"
I asked it, as I plucked each petal
But the daisy didn't want to meddle...

What Am I To You?

What am I to you?
Am I a jewel to be treasured?
Am I the recipient of your love
So immense it can't be measured?

Am I the apple of your eye
And the highlight of your day
Do you want to ask me when I leave you
Not to go but to please stay?

What am I to you?
Am I the same as you are to me
Is ours the kind of love
That will last eternally?

You Are Adorable

Adorable and enchanting
Charming in your ways
Entertaining and entrancing
Adding joy to my days!

Winsome and alluring
Full of so much fun
I love the moments I have with you
Every single one!

What You Are to Me

Have I told you what you mean to me?
Have I told you that I care
In such a powerful and wonderful way
About the time we share?

Have I told you that when we are together
I don't want the time to end
And that I know we have passed the point
Of being friend and friend?

I hope you know that I love you
And think you are the best
And I sincerely believe that our love
Will pass time's toughest test!-

You Are...

You are the object of my affection
You are the topic of my dreams
You are the glue that holds me together
You are the thread in my seams!

With all of my enthusiasm I adore you
And each day our time will reveal
That my ardor knows no limits
For you, I have unfathomable zeal!

Would the Stars Still Shine?

Would the stars still shine
And the moon still glow?
If I hadn't met you...
I really don't know.

Would the moonbeams
Shine and glimmer and slide
And would the Pacific Ocean
Look as wide?

Would the apple trees
Look as lovely in Spring
And would the birds
In the garden still sing?

Would the stars come out
And be as bright
Without you to look at them
With me each night?

Well, maybe these things
Would all still be
I just wouldn't love them as much
Without you loving them with me!

Meet me in the moonlight
Love me under the starlight!

Moonbeams on Your Face

I stand in awe and look at you
With the moonlight on your face
The soft and gentle moonbeams
Like the sweetest of embrace.

I see your eyes stare upward
As the fullness of the moon you see
And I thank the Heavenly Father
For His precious gift to me!

I can't promise you the moon
Or all the stars that shine
But I can promise I will love you forever
Dearest love of mine!-

Moonlight Becomes You

I see you in the moonlight
And I love the vision that I see
I love to look at your sweet face
At every opportunity.

It shines upon your skin
And softens it with its glow
So that you look like an angel
Stranded here below.

My Heart is Turning to Mush

I find that I'm liking you more and more
And hold you in highest regard
It has become so easy to love you
Where once I thought romance to be hard.

You are so easy to please and so loyal
And my passion for you has evolved
While the conflict I had over what we should be
I find has been neatly resolved.

I never planned to fall in love
And avoided the demands of a crush
But now I find that I adore you
And my heart is turning to mush!

Funny Love

Love is so funny
It is silly at times
It makes me sing songs
And makes me write rhymes!

It makes me spend hours
Talking on the phone
And thinking of you
Even when I'm alone!

Funny face, I love you!

When We Met

When we first met I liked you
And we bonded right away
I didn't have to search my mind
To think of things to say.

When I got to know you better
It became a natural part
Of our daily interaction
For me to speak freely from my heart.

Before long I felt as if
More than friends we would be
Soon you were my confidant, my soul mate-
And meant the world to me.

And then one day I realized
That the only thing to do
Was to ask you to marry me
And make all my dreams come true!

Being with you gives me such a rush

That I can feel my heart turning to mush!

Our Quarrel

We had a quarrel
We had a fight
I thought she was wrong
And thought I was right.

She said I was mean
And I said she was too
And before I knew it
Our romance was through.

Found out the next day
That we were both wrong
But the date was over
And all affection was gone.

When You Are Angry

When you are angry
You get a look in your eye
That hurts my heart
And makes me cry.
You make me feel better
When "I'm sorry" you say
And with your lips
Brush my tears away.

My Sweetheart Overseas

I miss you so very much
Each and every day
I feel so sad to know
That you are so far away.

Although the miles that separate us
Seem insurmountable at times
No amount of miles on earth
Can separate your heart from mine.

I do not know when you can return
For duty must be fulfilled by an honorable man
And I will be strong and brave
Though sometimes it is hard to stand.

But the things that sustain me
And will get me through
Are the gentle loving memories in my heart
Each time I think of you.

For that closeness that we felt together
Will not leave now that we are apart
For it is not a matter of miles that creates love
But love is a matter of the heart.

Our bodies are oceans apart
but our love is a heartbeat away!

Mom (as finance goes to war)

I watched you Mom as you stood so silently
And wondered what thoughts were in your mind
And I wondered what I could say
To show you how much I loved you that day!

Were your thoughts filled with the man
who could have been killed
And all those loving moments that would have not been filled
With the man to whom you became wife
And who became the center of our world...our life?

Did you think of me and that I would not be
If things had turned out differently?
Were you thinking of the horror that was war
And how different today's problems are?

Mom, I watched you then and I watch you each
time we are together
And I am always so very proud of you
The things you did then and the things you now do
I'm so very proud to have a mother like you!

I may not know what you are thinking
But I know that all those you love have a special part
Of that wonderful, warm and loving place
That is your gentle heart.

My hero—my love!

What is as Lovely

What is as special
As a brisk winter day?
You are more special
For you chase the clouds away!

What is as gentle and lovely
As a day in Spring?
You are gentler and lovelier
Than any single thing!

What brings such happiness
As summer days in the sun?
You bring more happiness
Than every single one!

What is as beautiful
As a day in the fall?
You are more beautiful
And more special than them all!

I shall love you forever

In winter or fall

But I think that in springtime

I may love you most of all!

First You Loved Me With Your Eyes

First you loved me with your eyes
Each time they rested on my face
It was as if in your eyes
Was love's sweet soft embrace.

Then you loved me with your arms
Which wrapped around me tight
And with your hands that held mine
As we walked in the soft moonlight.

Then our bodies became as one
On the night that we were wed
And I knew this moment
Was were my dreams had led.

As I look back and remember
Each moment had a special part
But the best love of all the love
Is that you love me with your heart!

Our first night of love

Still keeps me warm

In thoughts and dreams

Oh, sweet memories!

When Did We Become Us

One day I was "I"
And was content to be
Just the person that I was
Just happy to be "me"

Then I met you and you were "you"
And were perfectly content to be
Just the person that you were
As I was to be me!

But then before we knew it
And how it came to be
I was part of "us"
And you were part of "we"!

I'm so glad that we are us
And the two of us are one
For even though I still am "Me"
Being us is much more fun!

Love is where the heart is

No matter where you go!

And wherever it may be

I will let it show!

When You Hold Me

You hold me in your arms and all the while
Across my face is a happy smile
And my heart with love overflows
With love and joy only a beloved spouse knows.
When you held me for the very first time
I knew joy and happiness sublime
For I've looked forward my whole life through
To knowing the joy that is complete in you!

Why Do Willows Weep?

We walked today on a lovely path
With willows side by side
I did not know why they should weep
And their sadness they can not hide.
Why do willows weep?
I do not know
Perhaps their tears
Help them to grow.
I only know that
When I walk with you there
I have only smiles
And happiness to share.

Fairy Tale

I never believed in fairy tales
Never thought dreams could come true
Never worried about happy endings-
Not until I met you!

I felt like Cinderella
Getting ready for the ball
I had my own Prince Charming
So handsome and so tall.

I felt like the moonlight was meant for me
And the sun that shone from above
Was just for us to bask in and enjoy
As we celebrated being in love!-

Dance Me to the End of Love

"Dance me" she said "to the end of love"
And we danced the night away.
"Dance me to the end of love"
She continued to say.

"I cannot dance you to the end of love"
I said to this love of mine
"For to dance you to the end of love
Would mean dancing to the end of time!"

(thanks sis—you did good!)

Valentine's Day

Finding Your Valentine

Write the name of your crush
And place the paper inside
And to no one else
This name confide.
And then when Valentine's Day
Brings him to your door
You can tell your friends
That he's the one you were wishing for!

Cupid does his very best
And he isn't dense or blind
But sometimes he needs help
Finding your best Valentine.
So write the name of your crush
And put it in this box
And maybe on Valentine's Day
On your door you will hear his knocks!

Cupid! Cupid

Come my way
With a Valentine today!
Make him cute
And make him tall
Or just make him
not at all!

When We Were Young

When we were born
No one could know
How our lives would merge
As we would grow.

When we took those first steps
Each one toward a mother
There was no way of knowing
That we would find each other.

When we spoke first words
And when we smiled each first smile
Who could have known what our destiny
Would be in awhile.

Who could have known
What these little ones would do?
Who could know you would find me
And I would find you?

There was no way of knowing
That we would find each other
But Thankfully we did!

Two Little Kids

Growing up in suburbs
Cooking at each other every day
They were best of friends
And loved to play.

Two teenagers
Going their separate ways
Living close to each other
But avoiding each other for days.

He didn't want the guys
To think that he liked girls
She loved frilly things
And they lived in separate worlds.

Then one day his world
Turned upside down
She came to his side
When she saw his frown.

They talked together
For hour upon hour
He walked her home
And bought her a flower.

She read him a poem
And he sang her a song
And they found the perfect match
That had been there all along.

The Kiss

I gave her a kiss
Upon her cheek
And it was a moment
Before she could speak.

She wasn't angry
But she asked me why
And I was so flustered
That I started to cry.

"I love you" I said
And I blushed to my toes
But she leaned over
And kissed my nose!

She was six
And I was seven
But that day was my first
Little taste of Heaven!

Heaven smiled

The day that we met!

First Kiss

Nothing can be as sweet as this
When an angel
Gives a boy
A Kiss

Nothing can be as precious as when
Two little ones
Are forever
Friends

Nothing will ever again be as sweet
Nothing as precious
Nothing as neat.

I'll treasure these moments
And set them apart
For these are the memories
I'll store in my heart.

Who Set Our Friendship on Fire?

Who set the fire
Who lit the flame
When did it become so sweet
Just to say your name?
Who brought the flaming coals
And caused them to heat up again
When did our love affair begin
And when did "just friends" end?

First Love

My first love is still special to me
He brought such joy to my heart
While I was only a teen at the time
I felt we would never part.

He singled me out from all the rest
And just the thought that he liked me best
Sent chills of pleasure up and down my spine
To be someone's sweetheart and have them be mine.

My first love was an innocent love
Full of fun and flirting and joy
For I was just a teenage girl with a crush
And he was a teenage boy.

What fun it was to feel so grown up
And go out on a date or a dance
Sharing a kiss under the porch light
Was our idea of a budding romance.

Even today as I look back on my life
I know he has a place in my heart
For he helped me learn to trust in love
And our first love was a wonderful start.

First love, forever in my heart!

Too Quickly

Too quickly he said "I love you!"
Too quickly in the day
He should have known
That he would frighten her away.

She didn't know his intentions
And could not judge his heart
And from fear that he did wish her harm
She felt she must depart.

Take time to know the lady
Take time to let her see
That your intentions are pure and honorable
And you will win her easily!

Well...

Some men move too slowly
To win fair lady's' heart
They ponder and they stall
And hesitate to start.

While others go the opposite way
And jump in way too fast
And neither way is the proper way
To find a love that lasts!

Breaking Up Poems

Breaking up

Although my heart is broken I will carry on.
I will find someone else
To share my heart
Now that you are gone.

I thought we were a forever thing
That there would never cease to be
A couple made up of "us"
And forever a couple of "we".

I just need some time now
To look back and reminisce
To remember gentle moments
And perhaps relive our first kiss.

I will remember all the good times
And won't dwell on the sad
And for the loving times we had together
My heart can still be glad.

I am moving on now
To adventures sweet and new
And will take with me in my heart
The lessons learned from loving you.

I Didn't Intend to Love Again

I didn't intend to love again
I didn't intend to care
I didn't intend to allow any one in
Or ever offer my life to share.

I didn't intend to love you
Or allow you to love me
But one day you came my way
And you caused my heart to be free.

Gone was the hurt of the past
Gone was the pain and the fear
And every day now is a joy for me
Just because you are near!

I'm so lucky

And I'm so blessed

To have this abundance

Of happiness!

Starting Over

I will not waste my precious time
Worrying over the past
And questioning in my heart
Why our love didn't last.

I will not use my energy
Trying to figure out
Just what I did wrong
Or crying to "our song".

I will look back only to be happy
Over the joy I had
While we were together
And my heart will still be glad.

For in loving and trusting you
I learned that I am strong
And with or without you
I will go on.

Life would have been nice
If our love had been for real
And if our romance hadn't died
And we were together still.

But I believe with all my being
That soon my heart will see
That someone is waiting for my love
Someone who is meant for me.

How Do You Say Good-bye

How do you say goodbye
When you really don't want to leave?
How do you keep your heart from breaking?
How long do you let yourself grieve?

How do you learn to go on with life
And do the things you planned to do-
Doing them as one single person
When you had planned to do them as two?

How do you learn to love again?
How do you learn to trust?
How do go on living and loving again?
The answer is you must!

You must go on living
And enjoying life with zest
You must be compassionate and caring again
You must always try your best!

And someday you will look back on this
When your heart has had time to heal
And you will fall in love again
And this time it will be for real!

Love will find a way

To come again one day!

Romance

Romance is Wonderful
But is it wasted on the young?
A young boy should wait a bit
Until a gentleman he has become.

A young girl should be a lady
And appreciate the demand
That a lad has of being all grown up
A handsome and mature young man!

Don't Envy the Young

Sometimes I envy the very young
And the romantic things they do
But if I could do them all over again
I'd still want to do them with you.
We didn't have time or money
We didn't have fortune or fame
But we fell in love and stayed in love
And I proudly wear your name!

Young love only gets better with age!

Just Love Me

Sometimes you may not understand
A few of the things I do
And I may get out of sorts at times
And be a pain to you!

You might get tired of telling me
"Those jeans don't make you look fat"
Or even question my longing
For a puppy or a cat.

My parents may seem strange to you
And my housekeeping may be less than tops
And I may hit the breaks at traffic lights
And come to sudden stops.

My potatoes may be lumpy
And my hair might get frizzy
But just keep on loving me
And don't let things put you in a tizzy.

We will learn to live together
In a harmonious and fun way
And just think of the fun it will be to practice
Each and every day!

A Dream Can Come True

I dreamed a dream
And I wished a wish
Afraid just one
Wouldn't do
But my wish I wished
And the dream I dreamed
Were each that I'd find you!

If A Dream Is A Wish the Heart Makes

If a dream is a wish the heart makes
And a wish can be the hearts dream
My dreams and wishes should be one?
Or so it seems.

My wish is a secret wish
And my dream is a special dream
But one and both are the same
And to me they mean everything.

I put my coin in the well
And I wished with all my might
And I shall dream that my wish came true
When I close my eyes and dream tonight!

Dream a little dream of me!

A Little Bit of Humor in Love

To My Sweetie

My poetry does not gently flow
And I have no elegance in prose
So I just say as best I can-
I love you head to toes!

I Love You

I will love you in the morning
When it is time to awake
I will kiss you and wake you gently
And never with a shake.
I will hold you in my arms
And each morning I will say
"I love you sweetheart.
Have a happy day!"
I will cook for you each morning
Breakfasts that seem like Heaven
But until I get more practice
How about coffee from the Seven Eleven?

The Fight

My hubby is doing dishes
He is standing at the sink
He thinks that I'm mad at him
Because his dog pooped on the floor
But even though I was at first
I'm not angry any more.
He did the laundry also
And much to my delight
He remembered to separate
The dark things from the light.
Now he's taking the garbage out
And I really should let him know
That I'm not upset about the dog-
Maybe after he shovels the snow...

Never Go to Bed Angry

Never go to bed angry
Wise words my mother said
So we never go to bed
In the middle of a fight
Even if it means
We stay up all night!

Kiss me and hug me, no matter what the fight
It truly doesn't matter if you're wrong and I'm right!

The Proposal

I Want to Marry You...

I practiced and practiced
So that on our perfect day
I could wax poetic
With perfect words to say.

I wanted to rival Shakespeare
Or writers of world acclaim
When I asked you to say "yes"
That you would take my name.

I chose a ring with utmost care
To present to you, my Valentine
On the most wonderful day
When I would ask you to be mine.

I paced the floor back and forth
And up and down and then
When I thought about it
I began to pace again...

I knew that it must be special
And go down as a special memory
When we would look back and reminisce
About the day you said you would marry me.

But my heart just could not take it
And I trembled in my skin
Thinking, planning, pacing
Time and time again.

But soon the weekend was over
And I knew what I had to do
While all the eloquence remained in my heart...
I just said "I want to marry you!"

But thankfully, you, who are my soul mate
Heard the words that my heart could not speak
And blissfully I heard you answer "yes"
And I felt my knees go weak.

I know that in your heart you heard me
And forever, thankful I will be
That you listened with your loving heart
And answered yes to me!-

Always and forever, I do!

With This Ring

This little ring is a symbol
Of the unending love I have for you
I give my heart with it freely
For a promise of love from you.

As I place it on your finger
It fills my heart to the top
With joy and happiness
That I pray will never stop!—Thena

Please say Yes

I am a bit nervous,
This I must confess
For I'm asking you a question
And I hope you will say "yes.

It's a simple little question
And I've practiced every day
To ask you this important question
In the most romantic way.

So, I'm sending you this little card
Asking to look to the sky above
For tonight the moon is full and round
And I intend to profess my love.

Say yes, be blessed!

The Wish

I threw a coin in the well
What wish I made
I cannot tell
For the one thing I wish I knew
Is that my wish would soon come true!

Feeling Blessed

You Are Fabulous!

Y ou are so very fabulous
O h, how awesome and unique!
U tterly charming and creative

A mazingly you are so sweet!
R emember when I tell you
E njoy the days ahead

F ind pleasure in the little things
A nd concentrate on the good instead of bad!
B e aware of the others who are round about you,
U nderstand how people may feel
L ive life to the fullest and love living it
O nly worry about the things that are real!
U nder stress and hardship don't panic my love
S eek guidance always from the Father up above!

No Matter What

No matter where we are
No matter what we do
The joy of being your sweetheart
Always comes shining through!

I can see it in your eyes
And hear it in each voice
We are a couple by God's Design
This blessing was His choice!

Thank You for My Sweetheart

Thank you Lord for sunshine
To brighten up our day
And thank you Lord for my sweetheart
Who brings such happiness my way!

Thank for the things she shares
And for her lovely ways
Thank you for the laughter
That she brings to my days!

I hope that when you made her
You didn't throw away the molds
'Cause I hope that when you look at her
You say "I need more of those!!"

Loving the In-laws

Sister in Love

*I really love my brothers
And the sweet things they do
But the wisest and the loveliest
Was that my brother brought us You!*

*How lovely to finally have a sister
So sweet and dear and kind
To fill the empty sister place
That was in this heart of mine.*

*I am so glad that you are family
And each day I shall thank God above
For sending you to our family
Such a dear sister in love!*

A New Friend

*I always wanted a sister type friend
The kind of friend a sister can be
With a love that will not end.
And now my brother has brought you
Into our family home
And has given me the joy of a sister
A joy I had never known!*

For My Sister in Law

Your brother is my wonderful husband
And I love the wonderful things I see him do.
But among wisest and the loveliest
Was that he brought us You!

How lovely to finally have a sister
So sweet and dear and kind
To fill the empty sister place
That was in this heart of mine.

I am so glad that you are family
And each day I shall thank God above
For sending you to our family
Such a dear sister in love!

For A Wonderful Sister in Law

One always hopes and prays
That the one their brother would adore
Would not only be an in-law
But would be so much more.
I am so happy that you are the one
That came into my brother's life
To become my special sister
When you became my brother's wife.
God has blessed us so immensely
With a treasure such as you.
We thank him for His blessing
In the wonderful gift of you!

Happy New Year Sister in law
I'm as happy as can be
That you are in our family
And are a sister to me!

For A Wonderful Sister in Law

One always hopes and prays
That the husband they adore
Would have a loving family
That will bless them even more.

I am so happy that you are the one
That came into my life
To become my special sister
When I became your brother's wife.

God has blessed us so immensely
And each day we thank Him too
For the wonderful treasure given us
In the wonderful gift of you!

God bless you my Sister in law

I'm as happy as can be

That we are in the family together

And that you are a sister to me!

My Husband-Your Son

I look at my husband
And I realize
The depth of the love
I see reflected in his eyes

And as I gaze I know
That the love I see
Was in his heart
Long before he met me.

This heart of gold
And love of life
His joy over his children
Came before I was his wife.

You bore him and nurtured him
And taught him loving ways
You did the things that made him
The man he is today.

I see a wonderful husband
And the world's greatest dad
And I just wanted to thank you
For all the loving influence you had.

Thank you for your love!

Saying Goodnight

God Keep You Through the Night

Being with you
Is my delight
May God keep you
Safely through the night
And wake you with
The mornings glow
For God and I both love you so!

I Hug My Pillow and Pretend it's You!

I know it is just make believe
And may not ever come true
But it's so much fun
When day is done,
To hug my pillow
And pretend it's you!

Sweet dreams

My dear

In my prayers

You're ever near!

Wonderful Memories

*There's a place in my heart
With my sweetest memories there
While each one is precious
Some are just too special to share.*

*Sweet gentle memories of times of long ago
Of our love as sweethearts just starting to grow.
Memories of kisses placed on my cheek
Thrilling me so that I scarcely could speak.*

*I've stored in my heart for so very long
The sweetness of our every love song
I've treasured those songs that were for me alone
Those that were whispered, in letters, or over the phone.*

*I recall tender loving glances
From across the room now and then
When we were less than lovers
But much more than friends.*

*I will hold them forever
My heart stores them there
Sweetest of memories
Much too precious to share.*

Sweet Memories—of You!

Won't You Come into my Garden?

Won't you come into my garden
My sweetheart so dear?
The flowers have a little song
I'd love for you to hear...

Listen for their music
In the quietness of the day
Their leaves rustle in the breeze
In a sweet melodic way.

I ask this little favor darling
If this one thing you would do
Won't you come into my garden?
I'd love my flowers to see you.

Hubbies

Hubbies are wonderful
They bring us delight
And keep our house feeling safe
On the darkest night.
I'm so happy to have the very best
Who makes me feel safe
And so secure and blessed!

A Prayer For My Sweetheart

I pray for an angel to watch over you
To keep you safe and warm
An angel sent from Heaven
To keep you safe from harm.

I pray for you encouragement
When you are feeling blue
From friends with kind loving thoughts
Who will gently guide you through.

I ask for you sweet laughter
To come again to dwell
To heal that hurt inside your heart
That you know so well.

I pray that God will wrap you close
In His arms so loving and strong
To let you feel His love for you
And know where you belong!

For you belong to He who created
The earth, the land and sea
And He will keep his eyes on you
For all eternity.

Once in a Great While

Once in a while life is perfect
And everything goes as planned
It is as if God in Heaven
Is holding you by the hand.

Sometimes we have been impatient
And eagerly we've wanted more
And rushed headlong into adventure
Not waiting to see what God had in store.

Once in a while we listen
And do as He directs us to do
And the reward is oh, so wonderful
When God sends us someone like you!

Can You See My Smile?

Do you see my big smile-
The smile that lights my face?
Bigger still is a smile
That is in my heart's embrace.

I have this happy feeling
Just from falling in love with you.
Yes, there is a smile upon my face
But my heart must be smiling too!-

Our Wedding

Today we share a moment
That we will treasure all our lives
We exchange vows before our Father
That will make us man and wife.

How fitting that the seaside
Would hear us say I do
For as vast as is the ocean
Is the Father's love for me and you.

Higher than the tallest mountain
And deeper than the deepest sea
Is the love of our Heavenly Father
Who watches over you and me.

And now we say our vows to each other
As we look deep into the heart
Of the one we promise to cherish
And from whom we shall never part.

We do not take this promise lightly
We do not ever want to stray
From the vows we make before the Lord
On this our wedding day.

I Do, Love You!

Forever and ever, amen!

The Triangle

From this marriage is more than the two of us
It is made of not two but three
For to be a successful marriage
In the center God must be.

So I give a ring to you today
To pledge my love to you
And take the ring that you give to me
To be yours for our whole life through.

Celebrate!

We are here together
From near and far away
To celebrate with each other
This happy event today!

The bride and groom are happy
To see each of you attend
Ready to participate
As they each wed their best friend.

This is a chance to get to know
Those with who you will be related
And celebrate with the bride and groom
Who are totally elated!

Meant for Each Other

We were meant for each other
For we met and right from the start
We felt so in tune with each other
And you fell right into my heart!

We were meant for each other
For the moment I saw you I knew
That you were the person I was waiting for
To make all my dreams come true!

We were meant for each other
Not any one else will do.
For there is no other person I long for
No other person but you!

We were meant for each other
Our lives were meant to be one.
And though we knew in an instant
Getting to know each other was fun.

So now we face the future
Hand in hand as we go
Knowing that we will be together
And that our love will grow.

We were meant to be together
Together we will grow old and gray
Knowing that it was meant to be
And together we are meant to stay.

Prayer's Please

Please Pray
for the Bride and Groom
As you go about
Your lives each day
For the bride and groom
We ask that you pray.
Please pray for their spirits
To be calm and at peace
And that their excitement
And enthusiasm
Would never cease.
And please pray
For God's guidance
In each precious life
As they accept their new rolls
Of husband and of wife.

Celebrate! Appreciate !

It's Never Too Late!

Just love your mate!

Celebrate!

A Place to Grow Old

This is the home of my dreams
The place where my dreams come true
This is the home of my dreams
T'was my dream to share it with you.

This is our homey little nest
A place to include those we adore.
To rest and be blessed by those we love best
Which makes it special all the more.

This is the place we'll grow old
And where wrinkles and hair turned white
Won't matter at all for when they come to call
We'll still be a lovely sight.

This is our refuge from the storm
Sheltered by the Lord up above
This is the home that I prayed for
To share with my one true love.

Forever and always...

You are entrancing and fetching
So ravishing all the time
That I can hardly believe it
When I realize you are mine!

Seeing You Again.... for the Very First Time

I saw you only yesterday
And many days before
And every time I saw you
I loved you even more.

But today I saw you wear the dress
In which you would be wed
And it was as if a thousand stars
Went off inside my head.

I know I saw you yesterday
Precious bride of mine
But seeing you today
Was seeing you
for the very first time!

I saw you looking like an angel
A vision all in white
And it filled my day with sunshine
And gave my soul delight.

I will carry with me always
The look of you today
And it will a treasured memory still
When we are old and gray!

Til the end of time...

My heart is irrevocably yours!

First Dance as Husband and Wife

We dance as man and wife at last
With hearts full of love and joy
Waltzing and gliding around the floor
A dance that we both enjoy.

Held in your arms I relax
And feel complete for the very first time
Knowing that I'm held in your arms
And that you are truly mine!

Oh, God grant that we dance so sweetly
Through all of our married life
Comforted always by each loving embrace
As we dance as husband and wife.

But for now I am content to be near you
And dance this first dance with you
Preparing on this special day
To dance through my life with you.

A Glance at Wedded Romance

We have candlelight
By which to dine
We have a loaf of bread
And a bottle of wine.

We have a lace tablecloth
And as the music softly plays
The mood is set for the romantic evening
That we planned for days.

Continued on next page

Continued on previous page

I have on my lovely new dress
And he is dashing in his suit.
We raise our glasses in a toast
And our romantic evening begins... almost...

Suddenly we hear it at the same time
We put down the glasses
And we don't sip the wine
Baby is crying "Mommy, I up!"
We pick up instead her little sippy cup.

Hand in hand we go to her room
And we stand for awhile
His hand in mine as we look
And we smile.

Baby laughter and giggles
And squeals of delight
At seeing Mommy and Daddy
In the midst of her night.

She wants to play
And she wants us to share
All the happiness and joy
That she has to spare!

We share a look
A smile and a glance
And know for a fact
That this is true romance.

Bachelor Party Ditties

Some would say your fun days are over
And that your bachelor girl days must end
While others would suggest instead
That a real life adventure is about to begin!

We have come to celebrate with you
And join in on the fun
But those who are here with you
Are good friends every one!
So enjoy the fun and frivolity
And laugh and get silly with each other
But please don't do anything
That you don't want me to tell your mother...
Congratulations!

We are all celebrating
This special time in your life
While you are still fancy free
Just before you become a wife.
We will have a party together
And lots of laughter and fun
As you look forward to a new adventure
Before the month is done.
So, relax and live and laugh
And let's enjoy the time in a fun way
And then we will be there with bells on
To celebrate with you....your wedding day!
Let's have a party

The Wedding Alphabet

A nnouncing our wedding day , are we
B ride and Groom to be.
C hurch has been chosen and don't forget
D ate of the wedding has been set.
E ngagement is official
F amily and Friends are invited
G ifts are flowing in and we are delighted.
H oneymoon is being planned and oh
I love you so much.
J oined in marriage soon that will be us!
K isses and Hugs will be given galore
L ove letters will be keepsakes along with
M arriage Certificate and more.
N ewlyweds we will be
O pening the gifts from our friends.
P arents will be looking on and seeing our grins.
Q uestions and answers of how we met
R eception and dancing ...we will never forget.
S ongs played at the wedding will be forever replayed
T ossing the garten and the bridal bouquet...
U shers and Bridesmaids all look at us as we say
V ows to each other on our
W edding Day
X tra Special Memories and Moments and more
Y et to come
Z ealously, zestfully our life as a wedded couple has begun!

Weddings are Wonderful

What a wonderful day
Is the wedding day
When family and friends all gather.
They come to celebrate a legacy of love
That binds the couple together.

What a wonderful feeling of love
Abounds in the happy place
Where the vows are exchanged
Along with their rings
And then the most tender embrace.

Family Now

The bond of love is strong
And by these two we hold dear
Our families are forever linked
Each one of us who is here.
My brother is your brother now
And your sister is my sister too
Because of this couples faith
Who lovingly said I do.
I pray that our families
Will always be loyal and true
Not only today but every day
For our whole life through.

The Dress

It can't be just any dress
It must be white and feminine
And dainty as a petal
On the most fragile flower
Its memory will linger for a lifetime
From a ceremony that lasts an hour.
It must be tightly fitted
On the bride's tiny waist
And must yield softly to the touch
Of the grooms loving, gentle embrace.
It must also stir the emotions of
Each little girl in sight
Instilling in her the dream of someday
Being the bride all dressed in white.

Cutting the Cake

Symbolically they pose
Hand in hand with knife
And then once the camera clicks
They smile at each other
Knowing they are really husband and wife.

A year from now
They will relive this day
With a tiny layer of cake put away
And the photos in their hearts
They will replay and replay and replay.

My Bridesmaid

I'm getting married
And starting a new life.
Going from being just "me,"
To being someone's wife!

I'm getting married
And it is such a special day.
I'm glad to have my sister
Standing beside me all the way.

We've shared so many special times
Throughout our years together.
You have been my loving strength
Through good times, bad times or whatever.

So it is only fitting
Standing beside me would be you.
Supporting me with sisterly love
As you hear me say "I do".

A Bridesmaid is such an important part

of a special day and deserves to be noted as such.

For so many things, if you just notice,

Require her delicate touch!

Dancing With Mom

Here I am after all this time
Doing something that
I have never done before.
I'm happily dancing with my mom
Gliding across the ballroom floor.
As I feel the gentleness of your arms
And your hand squeezing mine ever so gently.
I know that to keep your eyes from releasing tears
You are concentrating ever so intently.
My mind goes back through the years
To the times you shared my joys
And when so sweetly and lovingly
You kissed my wounds and wiped away my tears.
It seems not to be the popular or manly thing to do
Being openly affectionate to a teenager's mother.
And siblings when with their peers
Seem to downplay their love for one another.
But I know that even in those times when I feel embarrassed
To tell you that you are a woman who I truly adore
You knew that I loved you every bit as much then,
As I do today as we waltz across the floor.
I love the gentleness and strength of your arms.
I love the tenderness and compassion of your spirit.
I love the joy of finally dancing
on this special day with you
And saying, "I love you, Mother,"
where everyone around will hear it!

A Thank You for Mom

Thank you Mom for being there
In good times and in bad.
Celebrating with me when I was happy
And cheering me when I was sad.
You have been my inspiration
And the one who cheered me on.
Your loving heart has nurtured me
And your intuition is never wrong.
This little candle is for you
And is filled with utmost emotion
To signify my love for you Mom
And my deepest devotion.

Mother In-Law

One of the greatest gifts
I have ever received,
Is something only you could give
And it will be my most treasured gift
For as long as I shall live.

On this day as we celebrate
The joy of our wedded bliss
I just want to let you know
You deserve a thank you kiss!

Little Flower Girl

So nervous and shy
She waits, basket in hand
She wiggles and squirms
Oh, it's so hard to stand!
Looking around at the people in pews
She scratches her nose
And she tugs at new shoes.
Then the music starts to play,
Suddenly she stands tall
And from her gloved tiny hand
Rose petals begin to fall.
She smiles so sweetly as she goes
Past the rows and rows and rows
And at the end she stops and sighs
As her mother so proudly cries.
The bride walks on the lovely trail
Blushing from beneath her veil
And remembers fondly amidst this bridal whirl
When she too was a flower girl!

Petals of Love!

Ring Bearer

What a lot of responsibility
Rests in your little hands,
How carefully you practice
To perform up to the demands.

How hard it is to be comfy
In your dress up clothes,
Today you look so handsome
But you crinkle up your nose!

The crowd is hushed
As you walk in so tall and straight,
Everyone is smiling
As you stand so patiently and wait.

You made the wedding so special
As you held your pillow so carefully,
And never let it slip
With a look of determination
As you bit your bottom lip.

We were so proud of you today
For the way you did what
Was your task to do,
Never was there such a wonderful
Ring bearer as you!

With this ring I thee wed...

From God's Balcony

Do you think that from God's balcony
In Heaven up above,
That mothers are allowed to view
The children that they love?

I like to think that every time
A bride walks down the aisle,
A mother who has gone ahead
Looks down at her and smiles.

I like to think she watches
As the couple says I do,
And is filled with joy and happiness
When she sees a love that's true.

If God allows this miracle
Of hope, joy and love,
Then you know that your mom will be watching
From Heaven's portals up above.

But should this not be possible
I know this to be true,
That God himself and all his angels
Are watching over you!

From Heaven comes the love!

A Memory Box

This is a special little chest,
Use it to do what it does best.
To hold memories through the years,
Things that bring you happy tears.
Put in this little box so neat
Things that bring back memories sweet,
And save special things for quite awhile
That make you laugh or make you smile.
Put the little souvenirs
Of your wedding day,
In this little chest
To remind you of your joy
And the way you have been blessed.
And the tradition you may want to start,
That on your anniversary each year
You add another little treasure,
To the cherished memories already here.

If you opened me up and looked inside

I know what you would see,

There on my heart in a very special part,

Would be words of love from me.

Love's Farewell

Farewell To My True Love

Do you remember (how could you forget)
The time and the way in which we met?
It only took one look for me
To know that my life's love and soul mate
You were destined to be.
Do you think it was fate,
Or perhaps the Lord above
That brought us together
And let us fall in love?
Sweetheart, you were my life.
You were my treasure
And making you happy
Was my greatest pleasure.
I loved sharing with you my life,
I loved the joy of having you as my wife.
I adored the way that you looked at me
And the gentle touches on my hand or knee.
You always knew just the thing to do,
To make me happiest our whole lives through.
The only thing that I would have wished for
Is to have spent with you a hundred years more.

A lifetime of love isn't enough!

Here are our best sellers
and our newest creations...

Written by: Thena Smith

Whispers : Passionate Poetry **NEW!**
Where's Thena? I need a poem about...

Written by: Linda LaTourelle

Love Lines:
Artistic Quotes for Scrappers and Stampers **NEW!**

The Ultimate Guide to the Perfect Word
(Vol. 2 coming Summer '05)

The Ultimate Guide to the Perfect Card
(Revised, coming in February '05) **NEW!**

The Ultimate Guide to Celebrating Kids Vol. 1
The Ultimate Guide to Celebrating Kids Vol. 2
(Coming in February '05) **NEW!**

The largest collection of poems & quotes ever created!

*** The reviews we have received in all the top magazines have been
wonderful! The feedback from stores and individuals is awesome!**

BLUEGRASS PUBLISHING
M A I L   O R D E R   F O R M

Name		Date

Address		E-mail

City/State/Zip

Credit Card #

Exp. Date	Phone ( )

Qty	Title	Unit Cost	Total
	Whispers : *Passionate Poetry and Words of Love*	$12.95	
	Love Lines : *Artistic Quotes Scrappers & Stampers*	$12.95	
	Where's Thena? I need a poem about...	$19.95	
	The Ultimate Guide to the Perfect Word	$19.95	
	The Ultimate Guide to the Perfect Card *Revised*	$19.95	
	The Ultimate Guide to Celebrating Kids Vol. 1	$19.95	
	The Ultimate Guide to Celebrating Kids Vol. 2	$19.95	
	The Scrapper Mom (Decorative Art Figure)	$19.95	

Send order to:

Bluegrass Publishing
PO Box 634
Mayfield, KY 42066

Subtotal		
Kentucky Tax 6 %		
Shipping *(Per Book)*	$2.95	
TOTAL	$	

Thank You!

Bluegrass PUBLISHING
www.theultimateword.com
270·251·3600